This Book belongs to:

ENJOY FUN RIDDLES WITH ANSWERS

Kids love riddles & puzzles. Riddles not only provide fun, but also help children learn to think and reason. they are one of the most enjoyable teaching aids for children, as they depend on the great passion and pleasure children feel.

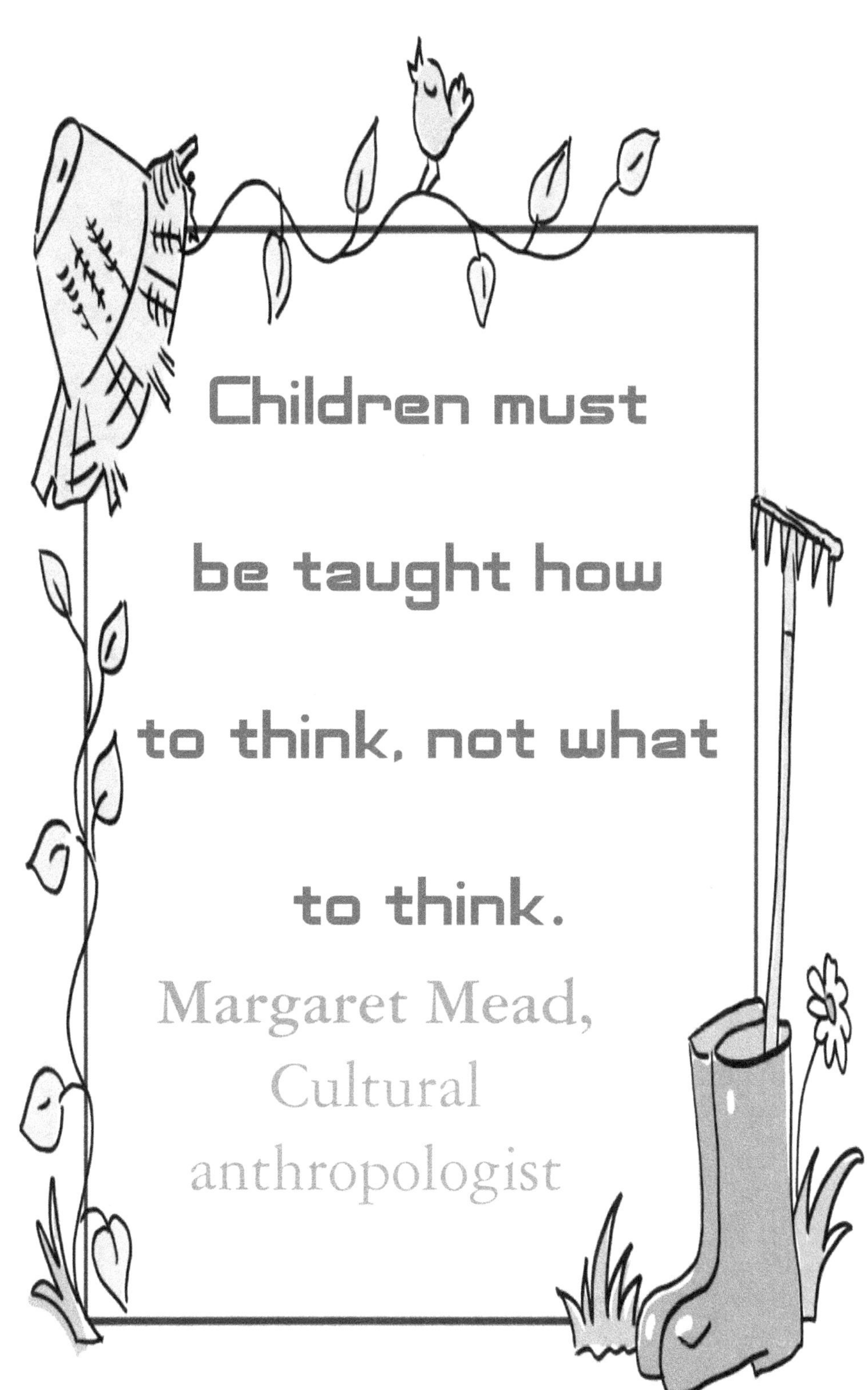

Children must

be taught how

to think, not what

to think.

Margaret Mead,
Cultural
anthropologist

Vince Gowmon
Author, Coach Counsellor.

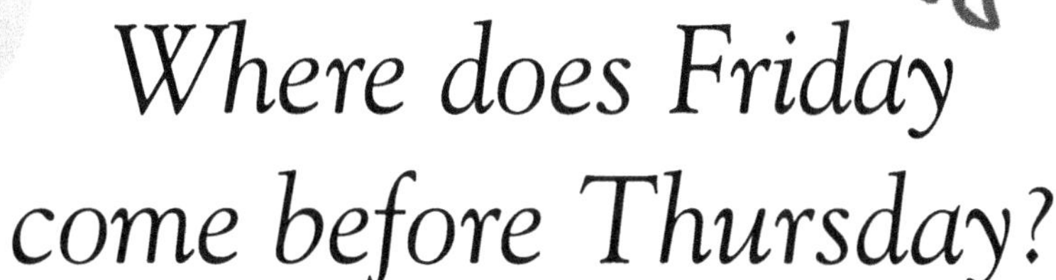

Where does Friday come before Thursday?

Answer: In the dictionary

What kinds of stones
are Never
found in the ocean?

Answer: Stones
that are dry

Why is the Mississippi such an unusual river?

Answer: Because it has four eyes and it cannot even see!

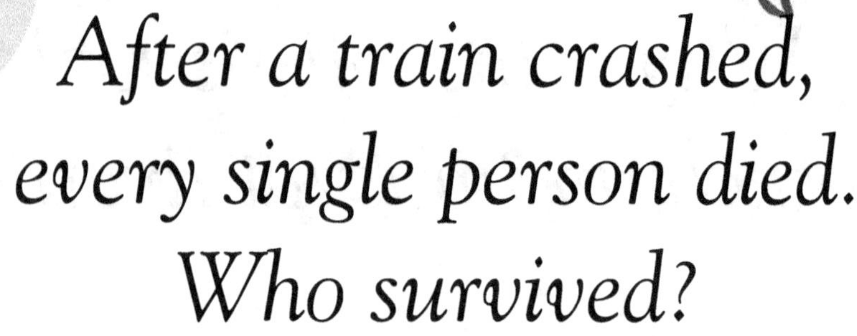

*After a train crashed,
every single person died.
Who survived?*

*Answer: All of
the couples.*

What goes around and around the wood, but never goes into the wood?

Answer: The bark on a tree.

How can you throw
a ball as hard as you can,
to only have it come back
to you, even if it doesn't
bounce off anything?

Answer: Throw the ball
straight up in the air.

Why was the broom late?

Answer:
It overswept.

Three men were
in a boat. It capsized,
but only two got
their hair wet. Why?

A little pool with two
layers of wall around it.
One white and soft
and the other dark
and hard, amidst
a light brown grassy lawn
with an outline of a green grass.
What am I?

Answer:
A Coconut.

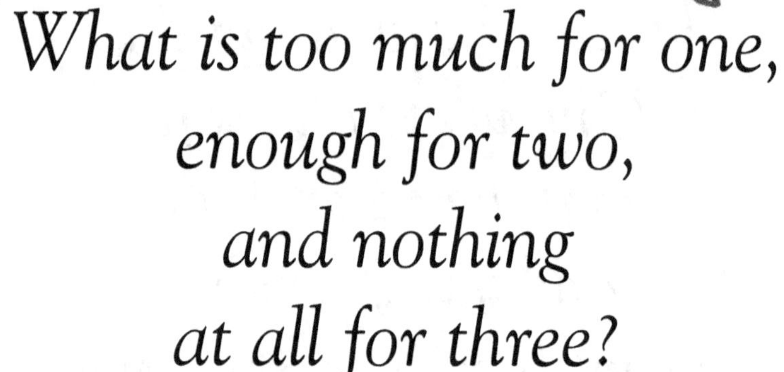

What is too much for one,
enough for two,
and nothing
at all for three?

Answer: A secret.

I have a hundred legs,
But cannot stand.
I have a long neck,
But no head.
I cannot see,
and I'm neat and tidy,
As can be.
What am I?

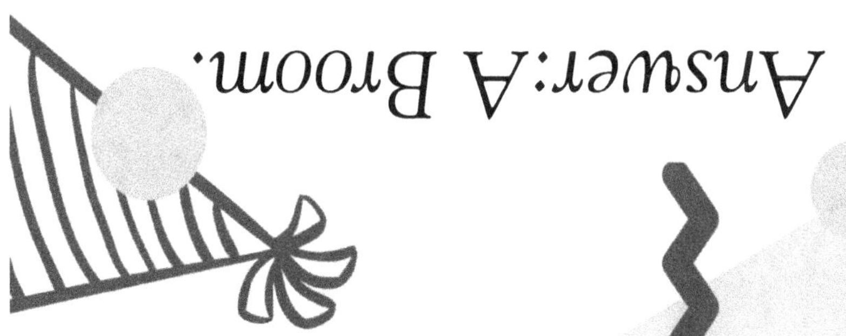

Answer: A Broom.

What is the best
present you can receive
for Christmas?

Answer:
A broken drum.
You just can't beat it!

You can break me easily
without touching me.
What am I?

Answer:
A promise.

What question can someone ask all day long, always get completely different answers, and yet all the answers could be correct?

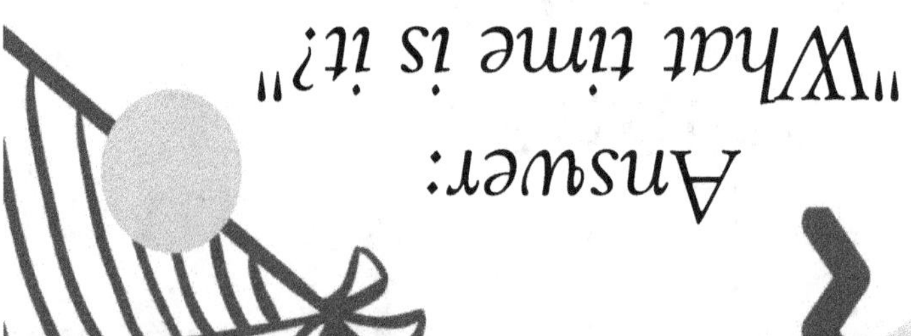

*Which weighs more,
a pound of feathers
or a pound of bricks?*

*Answer: Neither, they
both weigh one pound!*

*I have keys but
no locks.
I have space but
no room.
You can enter but
can't go outside.
What am I?*

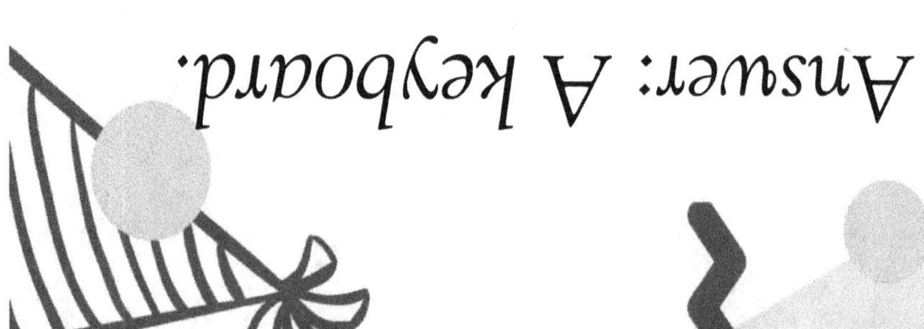

Answer: A keyboard.

What can be big,
white,
dirty and wicked?

Answer: A lie.

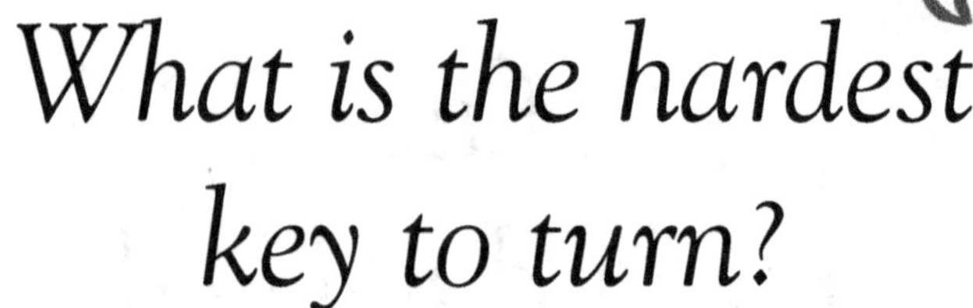

Answer:
A don-key

Why did the outlaw
steal the deck of cards?

Answer:
He heard there
were 13 diamonds in it.

I walked through a field of wheat,

I picked up something good to eat,

It was white and had no bone,

In twenty-one days it walked alone.

What did I pick up?

Answer:
An Egg.

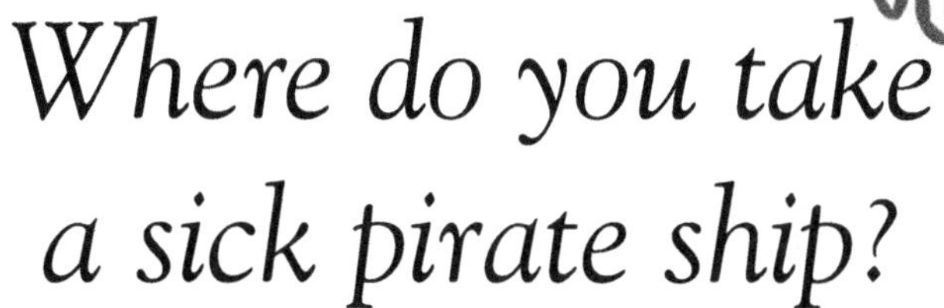

Where do you take a sick pirate ship?

Answer: To the dock.

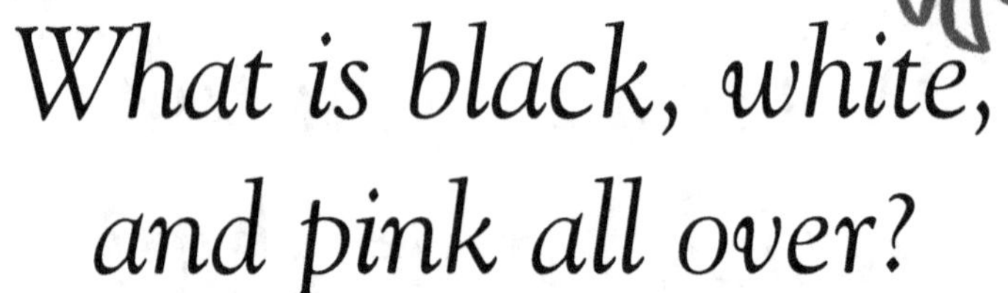

What is black, white, and pink all over?

Answer:
An embarrassed
zebra

What is the center
of gravity?

What begins with T ends with T and has T in it?

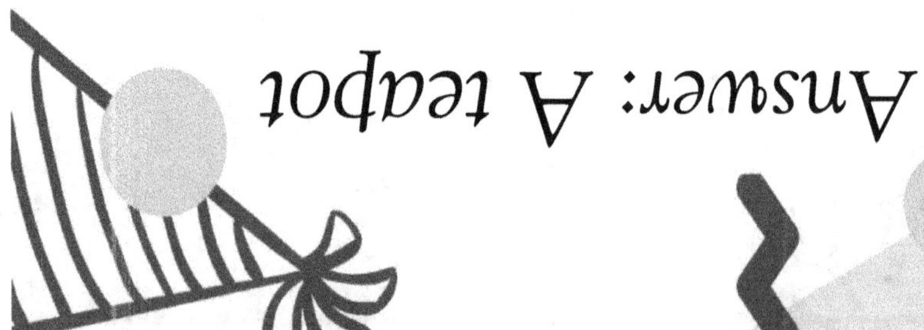

Answer: A teapot

Why couldn't
the sailors play cards?

Answer: The captain was standing on the deck

What is full of holes but still holds water?

There was a green house.
Inside the green house
there was a white house
Inside the white house
there was a red house.
Inside the red house
there were lots of babies.
What am I?

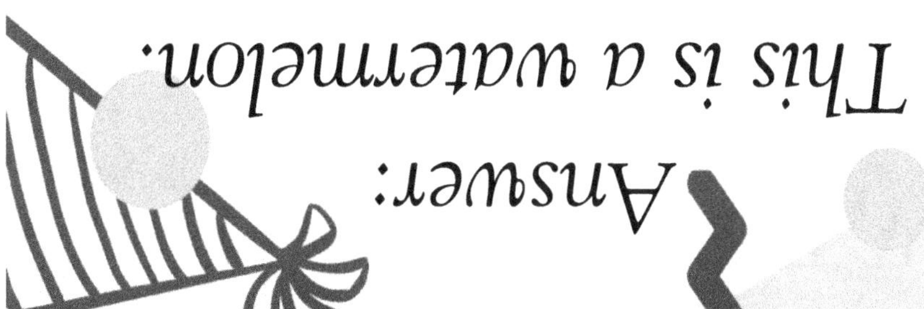

Answer:
This is a watermelon.

What can jump higher
than a building?

Answer: Anything that can jump
— buildings don't jump, silly!

I make a loud sound
when I'm changing.
When I do change,
I get bigger but weigh less.
What am I?

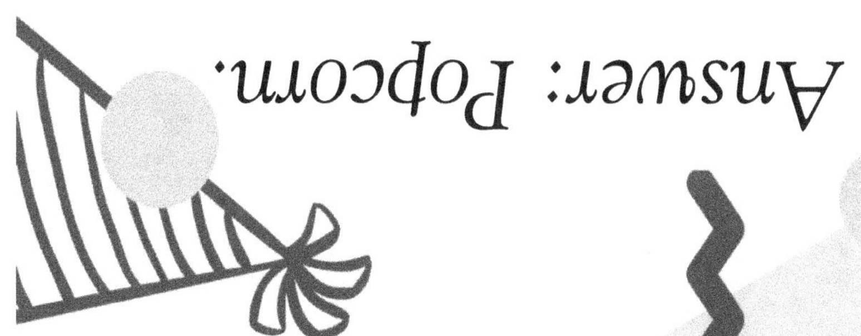

Answer: Popcorn.

Can not be seen only
heard and
I will not
speak unless spoken to.
What am I?

Answer: An Echo.

I am served at a table,
In gatherings of
two or four;
Served small,
white and round.
You'll love some,
And that's part of the fun.
What am I?

Answer:
Ping Pong Balls.

Sometimes I am born in silence,
Other times, no. I am unseen,
But I make my presence known.
In time, I fade without a trace.
I harm no one, but
I am unpopular with all.
What am I?

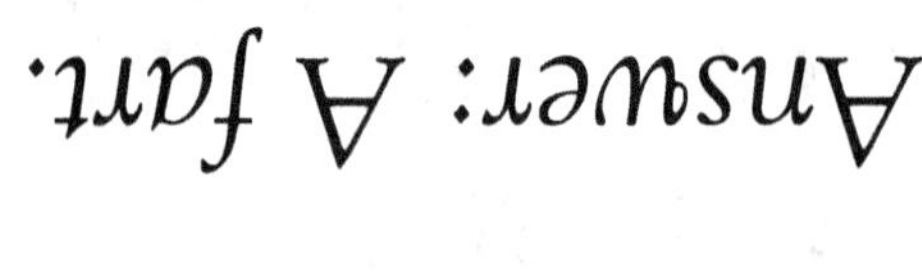

Answer: A fart.

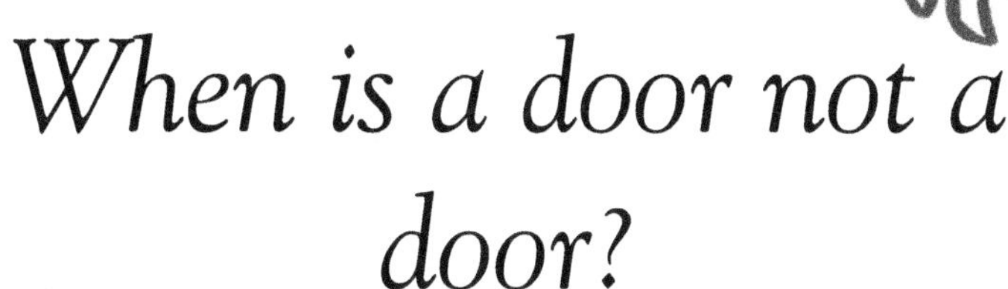

When is a door not a door?

Answer:
When it is a jar

What is as light as
a feather,
but even the world's
strongest man couldn't
hold it for more
than a minute?

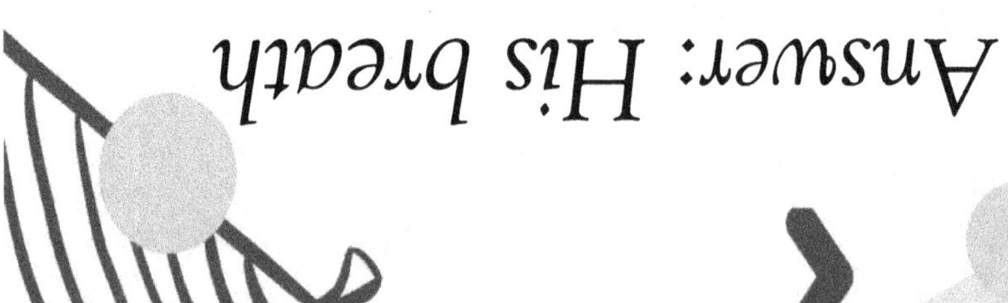

Answer: His breath

Which word in the dictionary is spelled incorrectly?

Answer: Incorrectly.

What bank never has
any money?

Answer: The riverbank

What has hands, but can't clap?

Answer: A clock

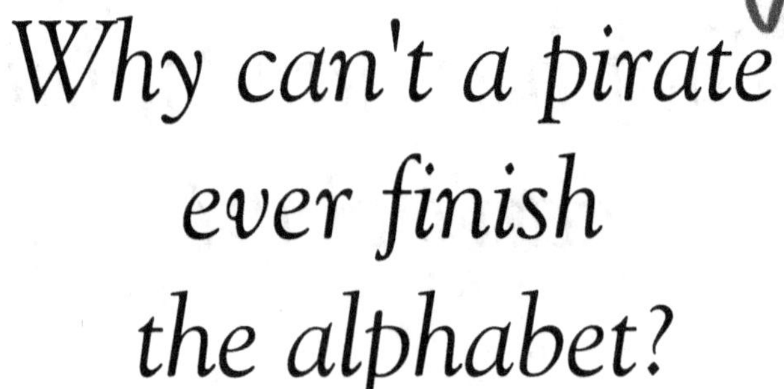

Why can't a pirate
ever finish
the alphabet?

Answer:
Because he always
gets lost at sea!

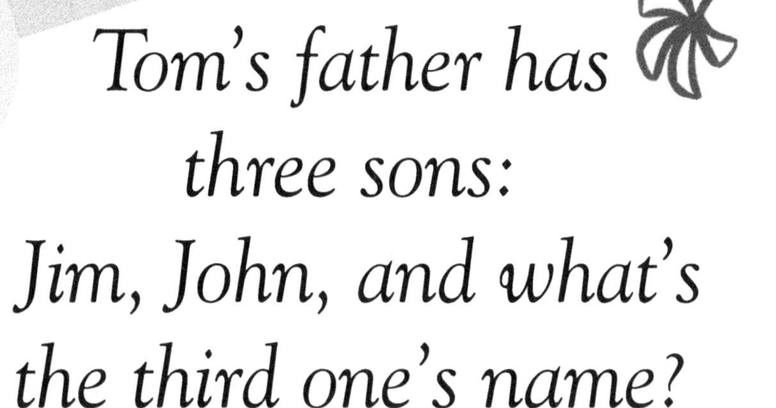

Tom's father has
three sons:
Jim, John, and what's
the third one's name?

Answer: Tom

What can you catch
but not throw?

I am an odd number.
Take away one letter
and I become even.
What number am I?

Answer: Seven (take away the "s," and it becomes "even".)

David's father has
three sons:
Snap, Crackle,
and ___?

Answer: David.

What goes up but
never goes back down?

Answer: Your age.

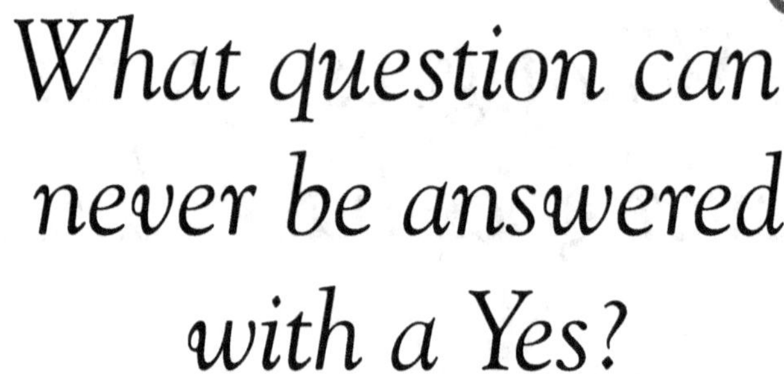

What question can never be answered with a Yes?

Answer:
Are you asleep?

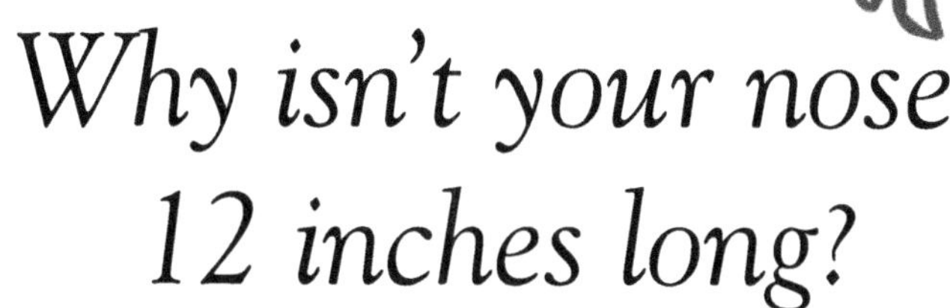

Why isn't your nose 12 inches long?

Answer:
Because then
it would be a foot!

What type of clothes does a house wear?

Answer: Address. (A Dress)

I pass before the sun,
yet make no shadow.
What am I?

Answer: The wind.

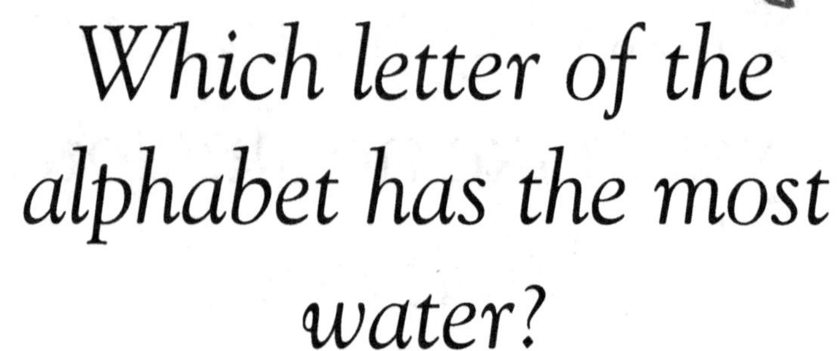

Which letter of the alphabet has the most water?

Answer: C

I have keys but
no locks.
I have space but
no room.
You can enter but
can't go outside.
What am I?

Answer: A keyboard.

What did one potato
chip say to the other?

Answer: Shall we go
for a dip?

*How do you make
a poisonous snake cry?*

*Answer:
Take away
it rattle.*

How do monkeys
make toast?

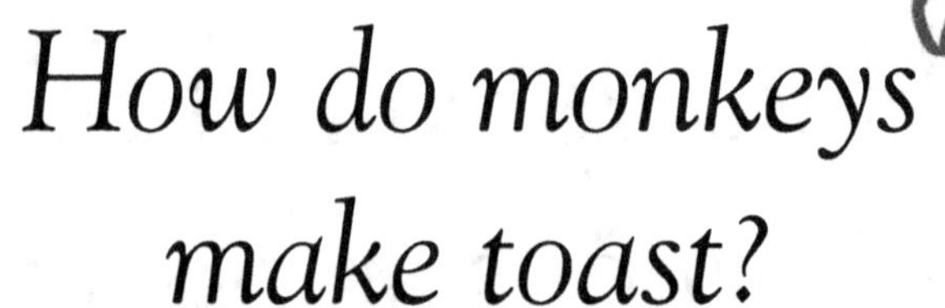

Answer:
They put it under
the g'rilla

A boy fell off of
a 100 foot ladder,
but he did not get hurt.
How is this possible?

Answer:
He was only on
the first step.

When I point up
it's bright, but when
I point down it's dark.
What am I?

Answer:
A Light Switch.

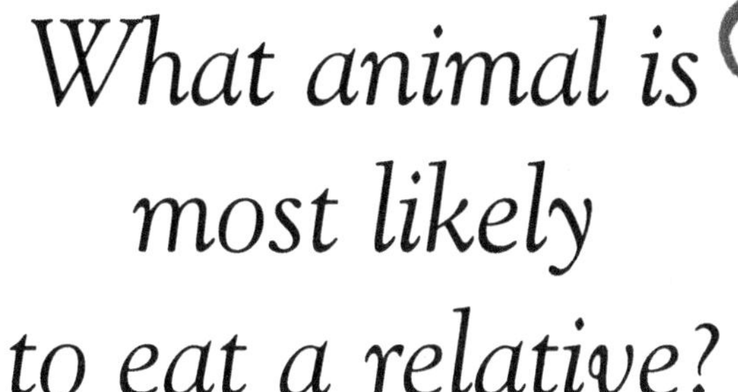

What animal is most likely to eat a relative?

Answer:
An ant-eater!

Where can you learn to make ice cream?

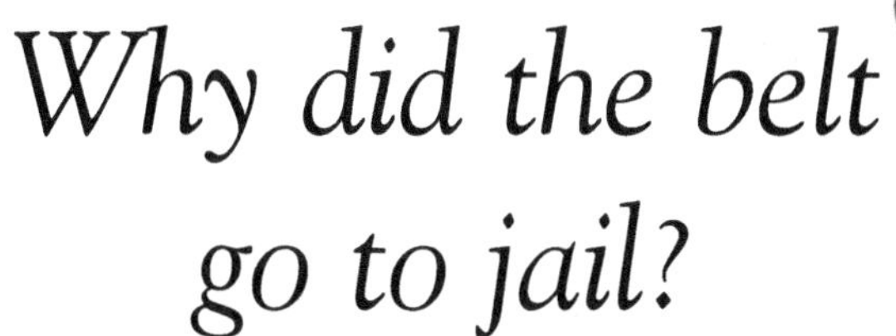

Why did the belt
go to jail?

Answer:
For holding up
a pair of pants.

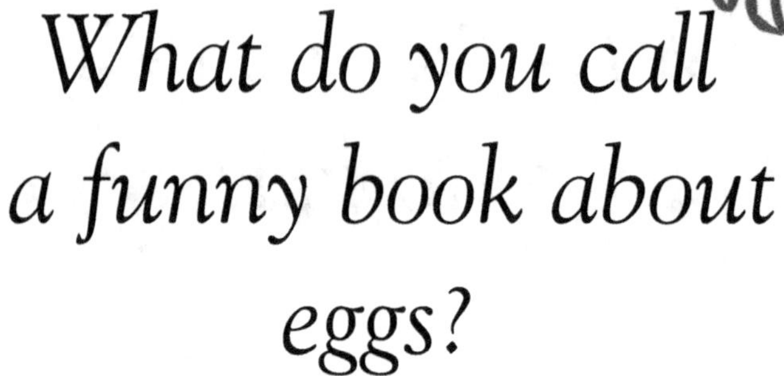

What do you call
a funny book about
eggs?

Answer: Yolk book

What did the beach say when the tide came in?

Answer:
Long time, no sea

In which month do
monkeys play baseball?

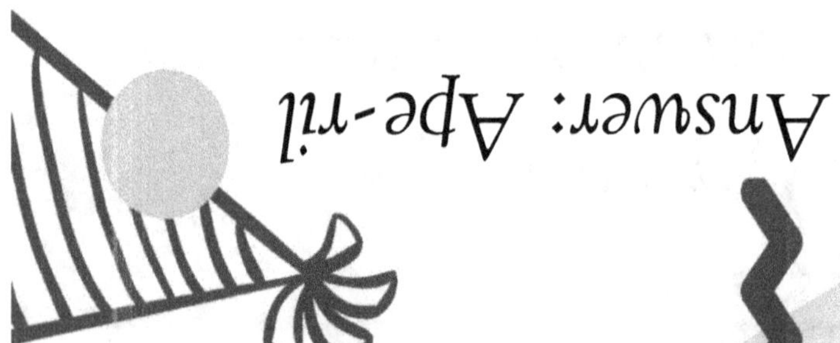

Answer: Ape-ril

What has many rings,
but no fingers?

Answer: A telephone

What has 88 keys, but cannot open a single door?

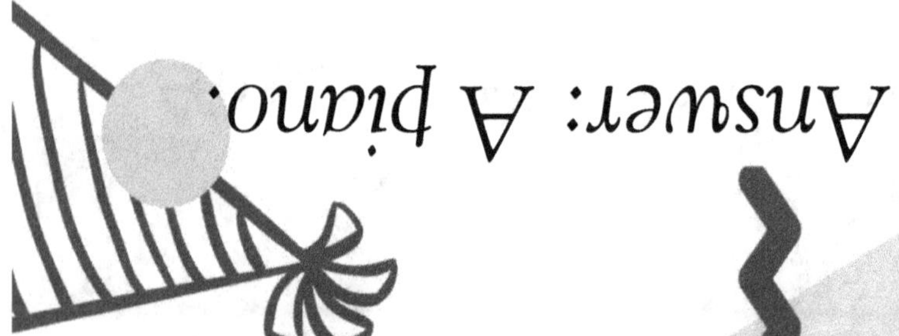

Answer: A piano.

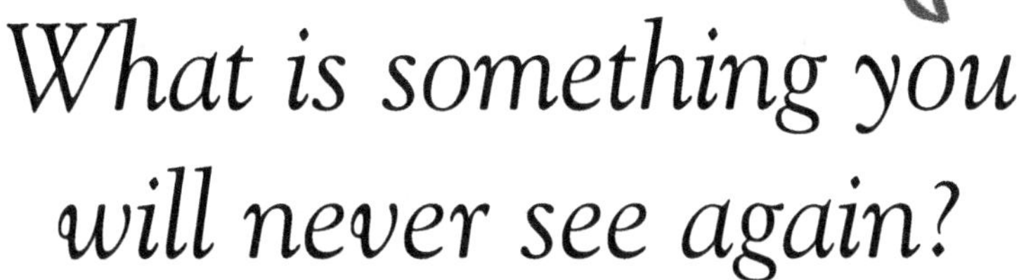

What is something you will never see again?

How many seconds are there in a year?

Answer: 12 – January 2nd, February 2nd, March 2nd, April 2nd . . .

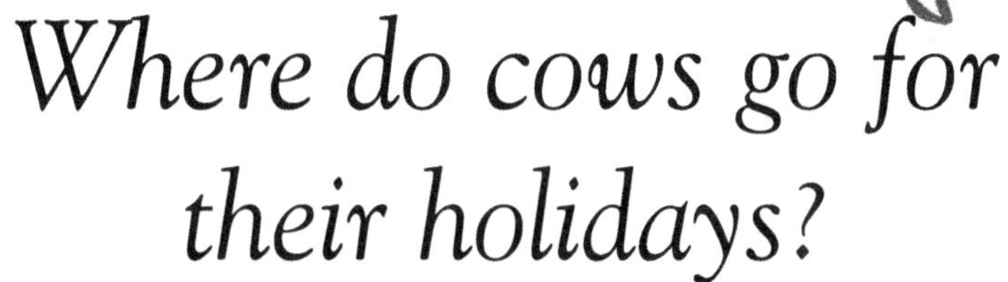

Where do cows go for their holidays?

Answer: Moo York

What invention lets you look right through a wall?

Answer: A window

What gets wetter as it dries?

Answer: A towel

Which month has 28 days?

Answer: All of them, of course

If an electric train is travelling south, which way is the smoke going?

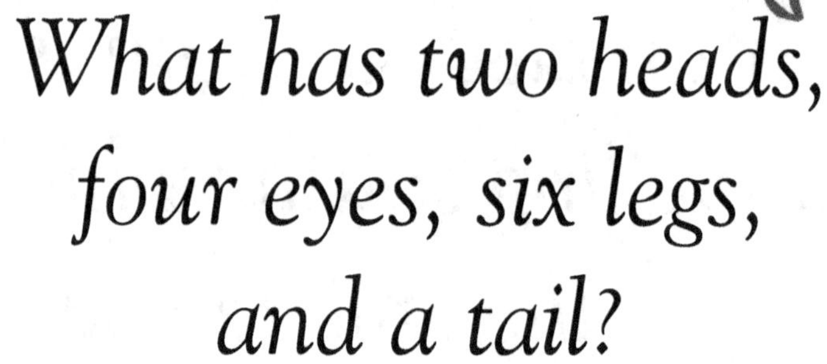

What has two heads,
four eyes, six legs,
and a tail?

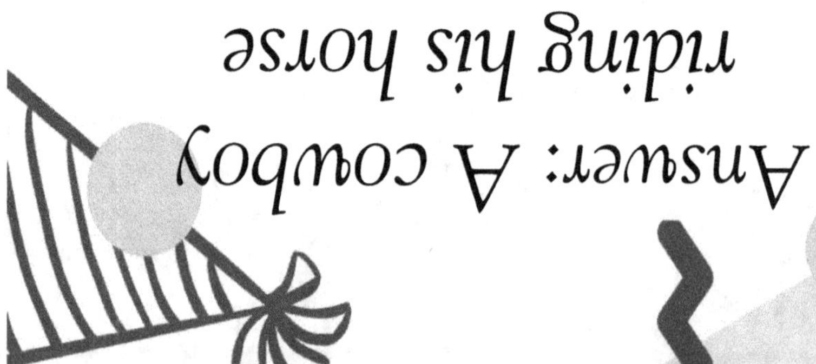

Answer: A cowboy
riding his horse

A man was driving his truck.
His lights were not on.
The moon was not out.
Up ahead, a woman
was crossing the street.
How did he see her?

Answer: It was a bright
and sunny day

As I went across the bridge,
I met a man with a load of
wood which was neither
straight nor crooked.
What kind of wood was it?

Answer: *Sawdust*

What is it that has
a bottom at the top of them?

Answer: Your legs

Why did the woman
Wear a helmet at
the dinner table?

Answer: Because of
her crash diet

What is the best cure for dandruff?

Answer: Baldness

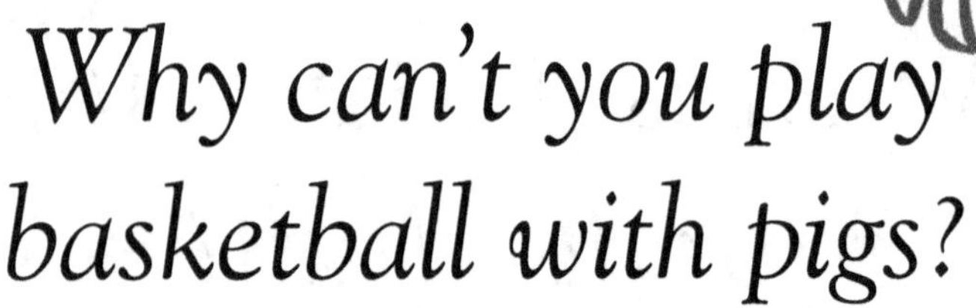

Why can't you play
basketball with pigs?

Answer: Because they
hog the ball

*Why didn't the hot dog
star in the movies?*

Answer: The roll was
not good enough.

What has a bed but never sleeps, can run but never walks, and has a bank but no money?

Answer: A river.

How many months
have 28 days?"

Answer: All 12 of them
do.

Grandpa went out for
a walk and it started to rain.
He didn't bring an umbrella
or a hat. His clothes got
soaked, but not a hair
on his head was wet.
How is this possible?

Answer: Grandpa was bald

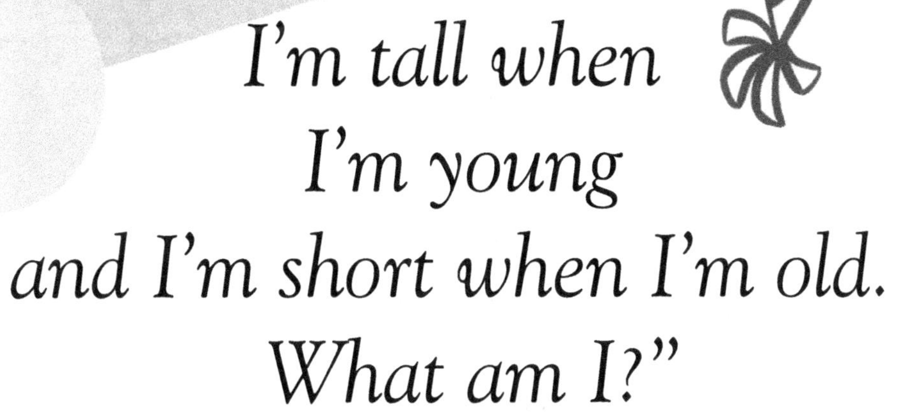

I'm tall when
I'm young
and I'm short when I'm old.
What am I?"

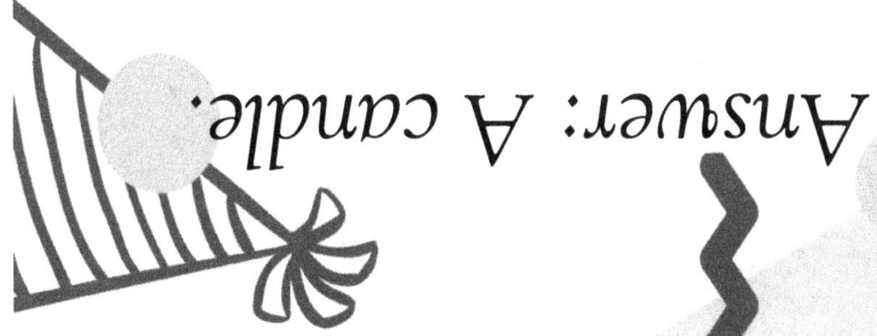

Answer: A candle.

I am always in
front of you and
never behind you.
What am I?

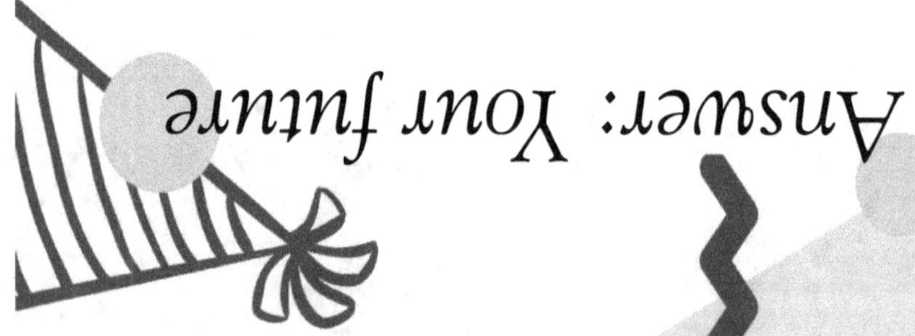

Why are ghosts bad at lying?

Answer: Because you can see right through them.

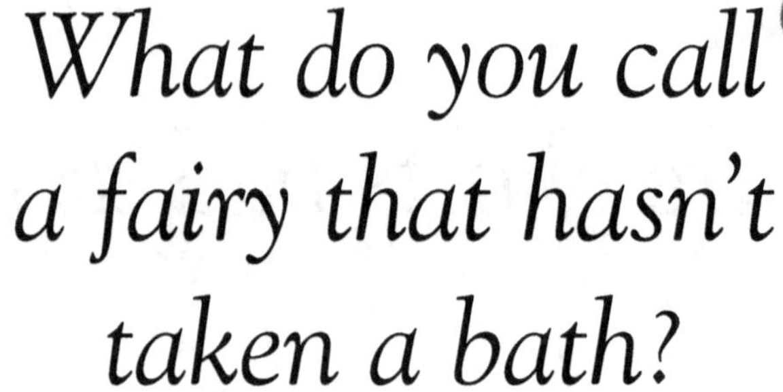

*What do you call
a fairy that hasn't
taken a bath?*

Answer:
Stinker Bell.

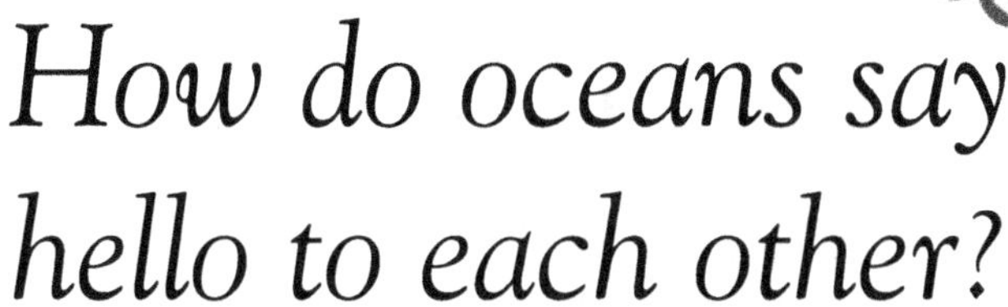

How do oceans say
hello to each other?

Answer: They wave!

Mr. Blue lives
in the blue house,
Mr. Yellow lives
in the yellow house,
and Mr. Black lives
in the black house.
Who lives in the white house?

Answer: The President.

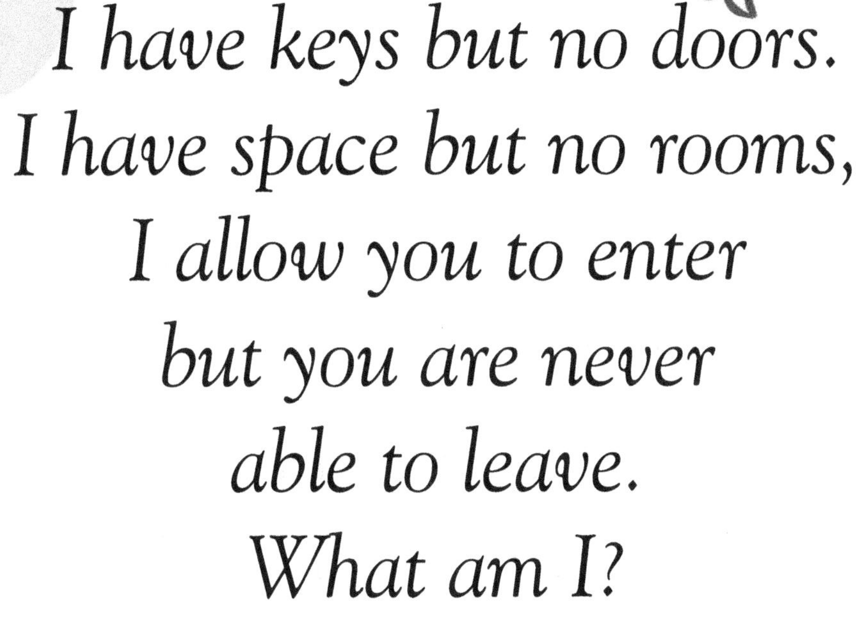

I have keys but no doors.
I have space but no rooms,
I allow you to enter
but you are never
able to leave.
What am I?

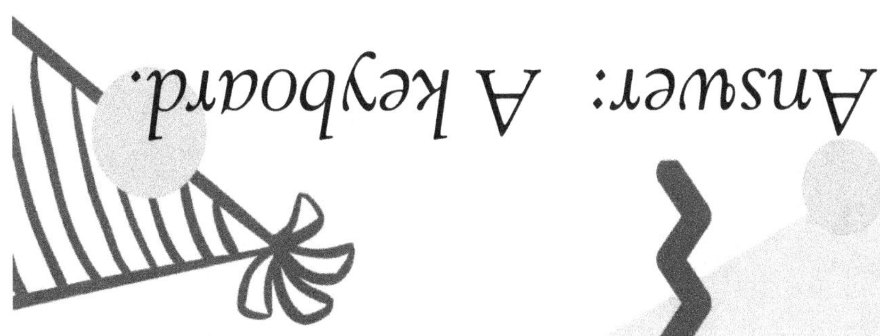

A truck driver is going
opposite traffic on
a one-way street.
A police officer sees him
but doesn't stop him.
Why didn't the police
officer stop him?

Answer: He is walking.

What belongs to you
but other people
use it more than you?

Answer: Your name.

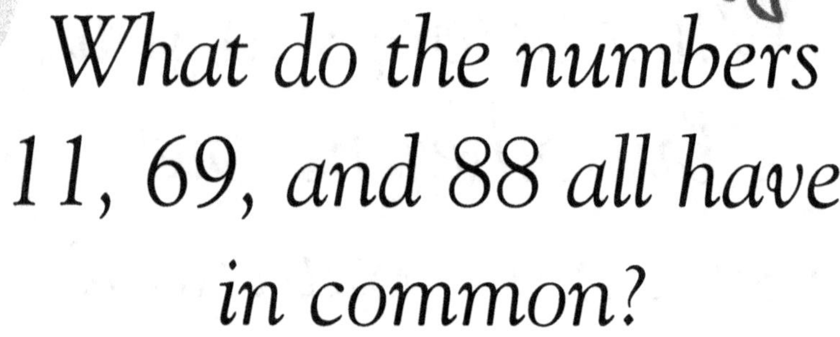

What do the numbers 11, 69, and 88 all have in common?

Answer: The read the same right side up and upside down.

If you multiply me
by any other number,
the answer will always
remain the same.
What number am I?

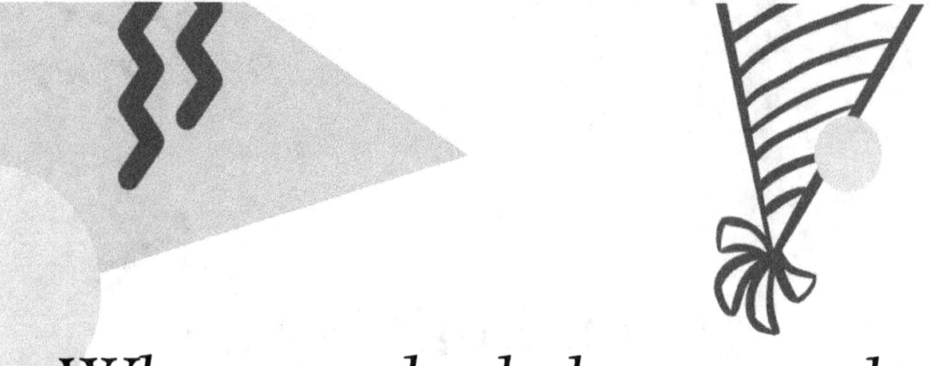

Why was the belt arrested?

Answer: For holding up
the pants

*What's black and white
and read all over?"*

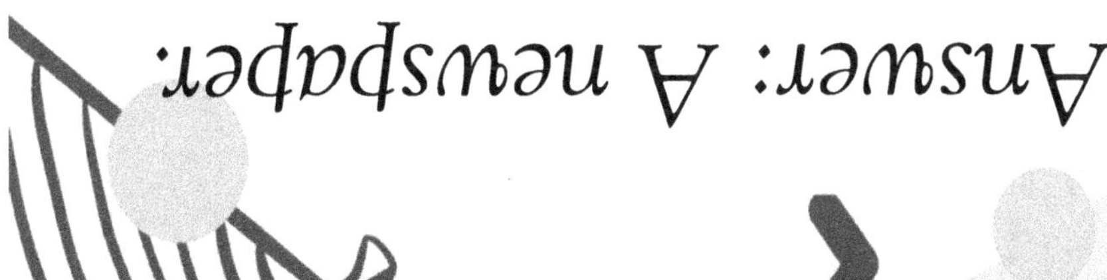

Answer: A newspaper.

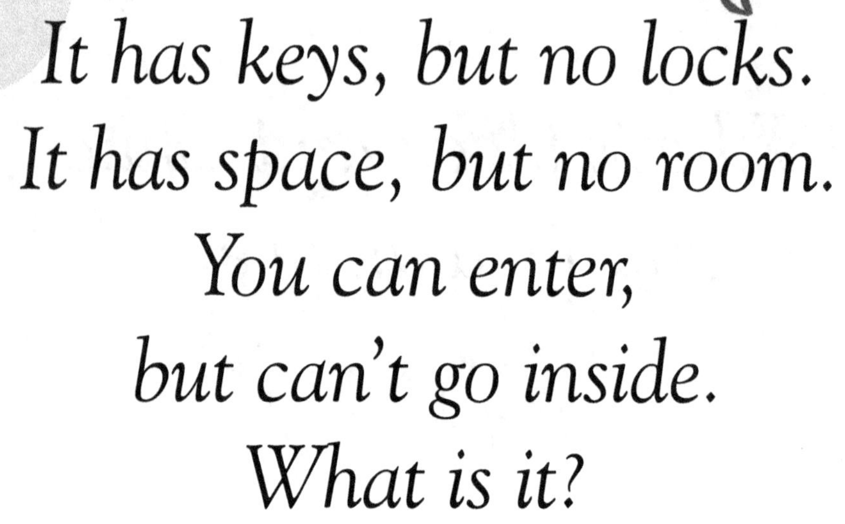

It has keys, but no locks.
It has space, but no room.
You can enter,
but can't go inside.
What is it?

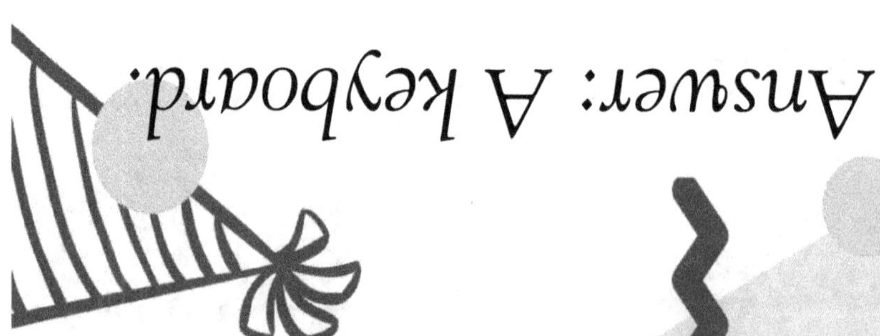

Answer: A keyboard.

What has one head,
one foot, and four legs?

Answer: A bed.

What weighs more?
A pound of feathers
or a pound of stones?

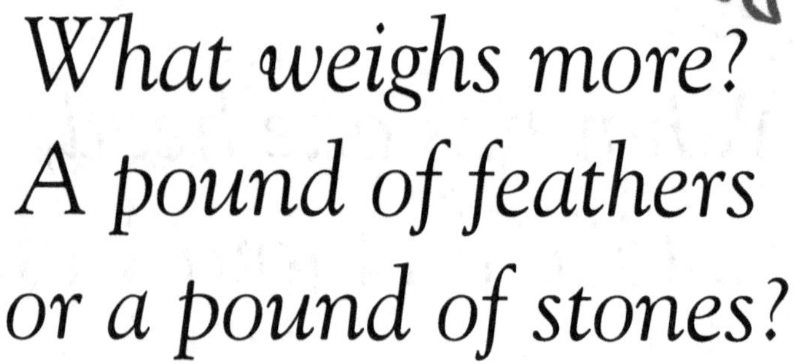

Answer:
The same. They both
weigh a pound!

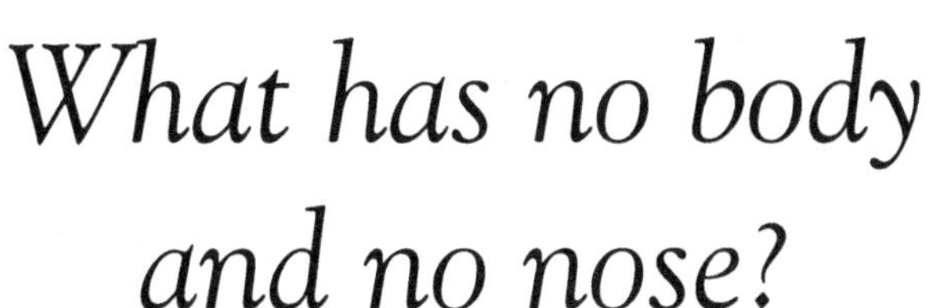

What has no body
and no nose?

Answer:
Nobody knows.

Who can shave
25 times a day but still
have a beard?

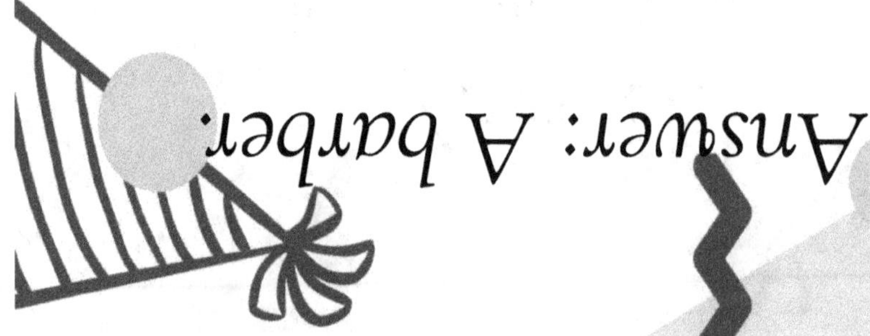

Answer: A barber.

If you don't keep me,
I'll break.
What am I?

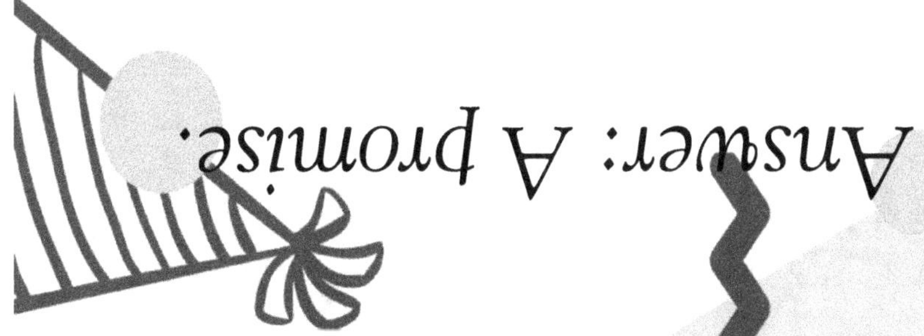

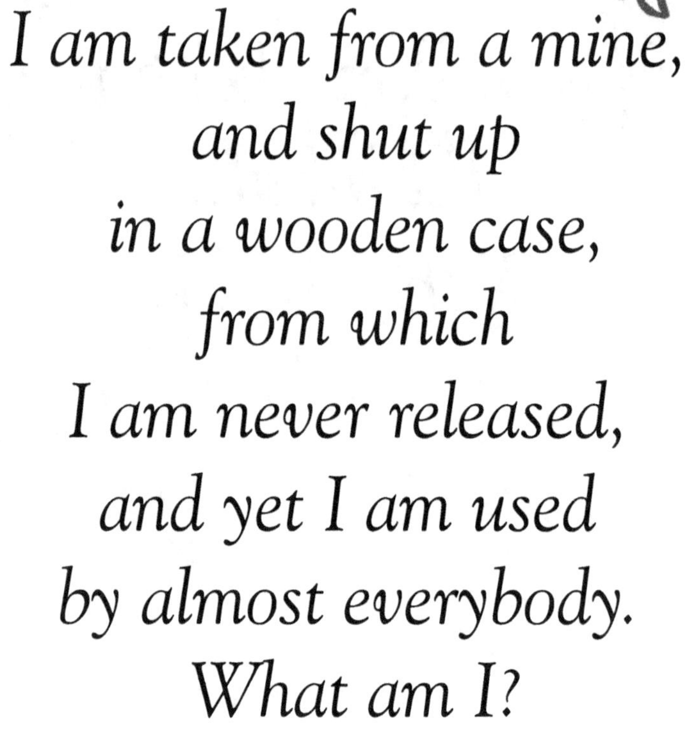

I am taken from a mine,
and shut up
in a wooden case,
from which
I am never released,
and yet I am used
by almost everybody.
What am I?

Answer: A promise.

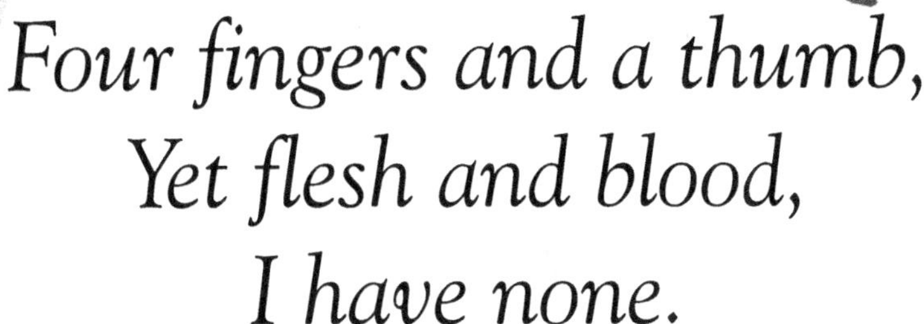

Four fingers and a thumb,
Yet flesh and blood,
I have none.

What am I?

Answer: A glove.

You can touch me,
You can break me,

You should win me
if you want to be mine.

What am I?

Answer: A heart.

www.ingramcontent.com/pod-product-compliance
Lightning Source LLC
Chambersburg PA
CBHW072103150726
47999CB00005B/1870